# Bugs and Plants Need Each Other

Cecily Jobes



ROSEN
COMMON CORE
READERS

Rosen Classroom™

New York

Published in 2014 by The Rosen Publishing Group, Inc.
29 East 21st Street, New York, NY 10010



Book Design: Michael J. Flynn

Photo Credits: Cover Patrizia Tilly/Shutterstock.com; p. 5 Image Source/Getty Images; pp. 7, 22 (aphid) Naaman Abreu/Shutterstock.com; pp. 9, 22 (lacewing) Christian Musat/Shutterstock.com; pp. 11, 22 (ladybug) PHOTO FUN/Shutterstock.com; p. 13 Alan Robert Jupp/Shutterstock.com; pp. 15, 22 (butterfly) chanwangrong/Shutterstock.com; pp. 17, 22 (bee) Daniel Prudek/Shutterstock.com; pp. 19, 22 (carpenter ant) Henrik Larsson/Shutterstock.com; p. 21 Lukiyanova Natalia/frenta/Shutterstock.com; p. 22 (background) jonson/Shutterstock.com; p. 22 (caterpillar) Brandon Alms/Shutterstock.com; p. 22 (grasshopper) np/Shutterstock.com.

ISBN: 978-1-4777-2302-9
6-pack ISBN: 978-1-4777-2304-3

Manufactured in the United States of America

CPSIA Compliance Information: Batch #CS13RC: For further information contact Rosen Publishing, New York, New York at 1-800-237-9932.

# Contents

# A Special Relationship

Emily's mom has a huge garden. Emily likes to discover new things that live there. She sees bugs crawling on many of the plants. Other bugs fly around the plants and land on them. She wants to learn how bugs and plants live together.

First, she learns that bugs and plants have a relationship, or a special connection. They need each other in order to live and grow.

Emily's mom teaches her about the relationships between plants and bugs.

# Plants Under Attack!

For plants, there are two kinds of bugs—the "good guys" and the "bad guys." The bad guys are called pests, or bugs that harm plants. Some pests are aphids, grasshoppers, and certain caterpillars.

Aphids are small bugs that have long mouthparts. They use their mouthparts to break into leaves and drink the juices. When there are many aphids feeding on a plant, the leaves may curl up and turn yellow.

Aphids also pass a sickness from plant to plant. Plants such as beans, potatoes, and pumpkins can catch this sickness.

# The Good Guys

Luckily for plants, other bugs kill pests. Some of these good bugs are lacewings, ladybugs, and certain wasps. Lacewings are tiny green or brown bugs with big wings. They lay their eggs on leaves. After the eggs break open, the **larvae** eat pests.

A certain kind of wasp lays its eggs inside pests. When the larvae break out of their eggs, they eat the pest and kill it.

Many farmers use special sprays to kill pests, but these aren't always safe. It's better to use good bugs, such as lacewings, to kill the bad ones.

Ladybugs are some of the best pest eaters. Emily turns over a leaf and sees tiny eggs on it. These are ladybug eggs. When the larvae hatch, they'll live on the leaves and eat pests.

Ladybug larvae are very hungry. Adult ladybugs will eat a bunch of pests and then take a break, but larvae will eat all day!

Before it becomes an adult, a ladybug may eat as many as 500 aphids!

# Protecting Bugs

Just as good bugs **protect** plants, plants also protect bugs. Many bugs lay their eggs on the underside of a leaf. Once the larvae break out of their eggs, they're safe and able to eat pests on the leaf.

The insides of trees are great places for laying eggs and making nests. Carpenter ants make their nests in dead logs and wood.

Bees make their hives high up in trees so enemies can't reach them.

Emily's favorite bugs are butterflies because they're so beautiful and friendly. Butterflies love colorful flowers, such as asters and Mexican sunflowers. That's because they drink **nectar** from the flowers.

A plant's leaves are important for butterfly protection. Butterflies often spend their nights on the underside of a leaf. Some kinds of butterflies spend the cold winter in holes in trees.

Some butterfly larvae are pests, but most are good bugs that live well with the plants around them.

# Pollination

Emily sees many bees flying around her mom's flowers. The bees collect nectar from inside the flowers. They bring the nectar back to the hives to feed their huge families.

In return for food, bees help the plants with pollination. Pollination is when a bee or other bug carries **pollen** from one flower to another. This makes seeds grow, so new plants can be made.

Do you see the yellow stuff on the bee's legs?
That's pollen from a flower.

# Breaking Down

It's important for some bugs to help plants make seeds and grow. However, it's also important for other bugs to help break down, or decompose, dead plants.

When a living thing dies, bugs and other tiny creatures break it down so it can be a part of the soil. This helps return important **nutrients** to the soil. Living plants use these nutrients to grow big and strong!

Carpenter ants chew the wood of dead logs to make tunnels for their homes. This helps to decompose the logs.

The garden in Emily's yard is like its own little world! At the beginning of the summer, there were pests on some of the flowers, but then the ladybugs ate them. The bees carry pollen from flower to flower. Everything in the garden has a purpose. Bugs and plants both gain something from each other. Emily thinks it's a beautiful relationship!

Someday, Emily will make her own garden.
She hopes there are lots of butterflies!

# Good and Bad Bugs

# Glossary

**larvae** (LAHR-vee) Insects after they come out of their eggs and before they become adults.

**nectar** (NEHK-tuhr) The sweet liquid a plant makes that some birds and insects like to eat.

**nutrient** (NOO-tree-uhnt) Something that helps people, animals, and plants live and grow.

**pollen** (PAH-luhn) The yellow dust a flowering plant makes.

**protect** (pruh-TEHKT) To keep safe.

# Index